♥ ♥ ♥

What's Love

Got To Do With It?

♥ ♥ ♥

By

NANCY M. POLLARD, LCSW

Published by
Benchmark Publishing, Inc., Park City, Utah, U.S.A.

Typeset by The Village Scribe, Park City, Utah
For information, contact:
Benchmark Publishing, Inc.
Park City, Utah
(801) 647-9202

CONTENTS

ACKNOWLEDGMENTS

♥   I want to acknowledge my sons, Brodie, Getty and Pablo. Without them, I would have never known true, unconditional love. I want to acknowledge my Mother, Dad and Brother, who have always loved me unconditionally.

I want to acknowledge my colleague and mentor, Paige Palmer, who always told me to not learn too much because it would get in the way of what I intuitively knew.

I want to acknowledge each and everyone of my relationships. You were perfect and precious to me, and taught me what I needed to know.

I want to acknowledge all of my friends, who over the past fifteen years have read many of my rough drafts, not knowing their efforts would contribute to this book.

I want to humbly and respectfully acknowledge each of my clients who found their way to my door. Without all of You, I could not have seen all of Me.

I want to acknowledge all of the great teachers who through their books have inspired and guided me. *The Course in Miracles*, Father Anthony de Mello, Jerry Jampolsky. Marrianne Williamson, Sondra Ray, Louise Hay, John Bradshaw, Dan Millman, Scott Peck and Arnold Patent... to name a few. I want to acknowledge Helen Lord-smith who reminded me that "this is what I know, I always have, still do and always will", and told me this project was not an option but rather a mandate.

I want to acknowledge Beth Kapp who typed through and above and beyond the hieroglyphics of several drafts. I want to acknowledge Lisa Ward whose efforts and talents at the final hour, edited and made this manuscript comprehensible, not just to me, but to the readers. Without her, I probably would have remained the only one who knew what I meant.

The highlight of my acknowledgment is to Ian, who believed in me and created the challenge of writing the Whole Thing, before I edited it. Without him, the words would have remained in my head, the details and logistics would have remained a mystery, and there would have been no deadline to meet.

And to you the reader, I want to acknowledge your search and journey to greater understanding and higher plateaus of loving, not only yourself but others as well.

Lastly, I want to acknowledge my dedicated belief and spiritual journey to God. Once "I found You, the search was over." May every word be what You intended me to say. May I always honor Thy Will and not mine.

DEDICATION

To My Darling Ian,

Without you,
I would have never known
the greatest love of all.

Nancy Pollard
March, 1993 ♥

All the names have been changed
and all the stories modified,
at the liberty of the author for
the sake of making a point.

You may see yourself in the following pages,
for our stories are the same,
just different names, places and times.

For I am you.
And you are me.
And we are all the same.

♥ ♥ ♥

AUTHOR'S NOTES

From my experience over the years as a psychotherapist, I know that many people are frustrated and disillusioned about their personal relationship problems. I wrote this book to clarify what relationships are truly about and *What Love's Got To Do With It*.

Single clients tell me that they are tired of getting their hearts broken time after time. They are afraid and apprehensive to ever get involved again. They want to know what happened, and why, and how to prevent the heartbreaks from happening.

Married couples think that they have fallen out of love, and want to stay married and get the loving feeling back again or get divorced, but find it difficult, or impossible to feel good about either decision.

Some remarry and are surprised to discover that the same old problems have surfaced again.

Relationships have a general theme that runs through all the case scenarios. The theme is Love.

♥ Falling In Love
♥ Falling Out of Love
♥ Loving Oneself
♥ Loving Another

Many people get stuck in the first two phases of falling in and out of love. Others progress to loving themselves and then, and only then, onto the glorious state of loving another.

To help illustrate the relationship phases and how to progress through them, I have used a compilation of case histories.

"I AM NEVER UPSET FOR THE REASONS I THINK."

This Course in Miracles lesson has been the backbone of my thought process in dealing with clients in my private practice in psychotherapy. As people share their stories with me, they usually discover that rarely are they upset for the reason they think. Their initial identified problem is often not the problem at all; which is why there is so much difficulty in finding the solution.

The stories unfold piece by piece, session by session. So, too, this book unfolds page by page. Problems are identified. Details are revealed and eventually we get to the true problems and causes, and then, and only then, can we begin heading towards resolution.

The process of psychotherapy can be compared to completing a jigsaw puzzle. Not everything is completed at once. Not every piece has an obvious and immediate fit, but gradually, the puzzle comes together into a clear picture.

Love is a bit of a jigsaw puzzle for most people with whom I work. It certainly was for two couples whom I have called Jackie and Jim, and Katherine and Ken. Likewise, the reader will meet Cathy, Bill, Melanie, Robin, Max, Tom, Rebecca, Suzanne, Paul, and more.

As their stories unfold, we learn that they are not upset for the reasons they think. And in the language of the Course in Miracles:

- ♥ they are not victims of the world they see;
- ♥ they can be determined to see the world (love) differently; and,
- ♥ they can lovingly release their past through a deeper understanding of the bigger picture of love.

This book shares love stories and stories of love. It explains and gives answers to loving. Knowing how to stay out of the vicious heartbreaking cycle of falling in and out of love, frees us to open our hearts to a different way of loving.

"All my life, I thought I knew what love was. I either had too much of it, or not enough.

I fell in love many times.
And fell out of love just as many.

What I thought was love, was not.
What I thought was not, was.

I thought I knew what I was looking for.
And when I found it, it was not.

And what I did not look for, I found.
And it was.

I didn't know, that I didn't know.
I didn't know that I was "asleep."

It was only when I awoke, that I knew.
What I didn't know.

I forgave myself for being asleep.
And I forgave everyone else as well.

And I knew that I did the best that I could
at the time.
And so had they.

We were just asleep, that is all."

PROLOGUE

The Beginning To...
A Long, Long, Story

THEY sat on the mountaintop. HE sat beside her. SHE told him what SHE knew. HE listened and asked questions. HE was very curious about all that SHE knew. SHE was very eager to share and was bursting with knowledge and truths. SHE had felt like the sun without shine... or the water without fall. The two went together and made the other create into another purpose.

SHE was conscious and fully awake to loving, trying to learn how to live in an unconscious or sleeping, unloving world. HE was in an unconscious, sleeping world trying to learn how to remember to wake up.

THEY have travelled many lives and many lifetimes to reach each other. THEY had come from opposite sides of the continent and THEY had met and both wanted a committed and pure loving partnership.

THEY wanted to stop loving from survival and begin loving from a place where THEY could flourish. For this THEY needed a partner. Not just ANY partner, but rather a partner who wanted the same thing, at the same time, and from the same person that wanted it too.

THEY had met others who had wanted to love them, but THEY did not want love from the ones that wanted to love them... and often the ones THEY wanted to love, did not want love from them.

Timing.

It all boiled down to timing. HE and SHE were about timing. All relationships were about timing.
SHE reminded him of that and also that every person THEY had had a relationship with had been a teacher. SHE reminded him as well that when we have learned all that we can learn from a relationship, then we move on to the next. And sometimes we stay with relationships because there is still more to learn.
HE and SHE had a lot to learn and only together as THEY, could THEY grow into synergistic partners, awake and fully conscious of loving. THEY wanted to learn about being together as individuals and being more than THEY could be on their own.

End of the Beginning to a... Long, Long, Story.

INTRODUCTION

A Short Story

In Love

One day when I was young, I looked up and saw a very tall mountain. I wanted very much to climb that mountain but believed that I could never do so alone. I fantasized and prayed that someday, someone, would come along and lead me to the top. That day came, and he led me to the top and we had a glorious time on the way up. We giggled and laughed, and played and struggled, and finally reached the top together. It was great and I was grateful and everyday, I thanked him.

I called this in love.

Out of Love

Then one day, I decided to go down the mountain and then back up the mountain by myself. I wanted desperately to prove to myself that I could do it... all by myself. *This I did, over and over and over again. I began to resent that he wanted to show me the way, when I had discovered my own way to climb it. I told him I didn't want to climb the mountain HIS way. I wanted to climb it MY way, and to go away and to leave me alone. This he did.*

I called this out of love.

Loving Myself

For many years, I climbed the mountain all by myself. Sometimes I would see the sunset, and sometimes I would see the sunrise. Sometimes I would prepare myself a big feast on top of the mountain... and I would enjoy it and feel proud.

I called this loving myself.

Loving Another

After many years of doing this alone, I realized that maybe there was more. Maybe it would be nice to share the beautiful sunset and sumptuous meal with another. I did not want to bring someone up my way, but rather, I wanted him to find his own way and be at the top with me.

And one day, with a back pack filled with drink and food, I hiked my mountain and when I reached the top I leaned against a tree.

Directly behind me, sat a man. He had come up on the other side of the mountain. He had traveled the path to the top many times, not only on his own, but he had shown many women the way as well. He had grown weary of being the leader and wished that someday, he would find someone that had found their own way to the top. He had much to tell me about his path, his way and his travels. As well, he was very curious about my path, my way, and my travels. Together, we shared our stories and our food and watched the sunset. Sharing the beauty and each other was more than I could ever experience alone.

I called this loving another.

♥ ♥ ♥

♥   ♥   ♥

Falling

In

Love

♥   ♥   ♥

"I love you."

"I love you, too."

Magical words. We say them and we want to hear them back. And when and if we do, we determine that we are in love! It is a wonderful feeling. Whether we hear these words for the first time at age sixteen or again at age sixty, the feeling is the same. All of us at some time in our lives have fallen in love at least once, maybe even several times.

Chances are high that if we have fallen *in love*, we have fallen *out of love*. The processes of falling in love and falling out of love each affect our lives dramatically. Although, one is positive and the other negative, they are equally powerful. We can easily conjure up the feeling and the thrill that falling in love solicits. Likewise, the pain and the agony of a broken heart, remains for some throughout a lifetime.

What is interesting is that we think we know what love is and what it is not.

♥ *OR DO WE?*

What is it all about... falling in love? What makes us fall in love and then what makes us fall out of love?

To illustrate falling in love and out of love, we will follow the stories of two couples: Jackie and Jim, and Katherine and Ken. We will piece together the jigsaw puzzle of their lives, slowly coming to understand the true motivation that drives each individual's need for love. We will explore why, when, and how these individuals fall in love, out of love, and come to love themselves and love another again.

♥ *JACKIE AND JIM*

Jackie's Story

Jackie's story was right out of the Fairy Tales.

"He was everything... he was wonderful. He was a dream come true. I used to call him my Prince Charming. He was handsome, had a great body, a tan, and was very athletic. He was the captain of the football team and president of the student body. Everyone wanted to go out with him. He had a mind of his own and most of all, he was going to be somebody in his life... a doer, not a talker. He wanted to be a big shot and make lots of money. He was a natural born salesman. He could sell anything. He was a charmer all right.
And one day, out of the blue, like magic, he called me. I couldn't believe it. I had never had a "boyfriend". I was everybody's friend, but no-body's "girlfriend". I got straight A's and I guess people thought I was nerdy.
Mother had warned me not to blow it with him because, as she said many times, "guys like this don't come along everyday". She took me shopping for new clothes so that I wouldn't look so square. Dad didn't like him very much, but Mother said Dad was jealous and intimidated by his charm and big plans. He was so wonderful. So perfect. I knew that if I married him, I would never feel

ashamed, like Mother had, of not having money and nice things. "

Jackie told me this story amidst tears of sentimentality, grief and dismay. She described the beginning of a classic dependent relationship, of a young and naive woman's attachment to a man who could give her security and an identity, i.e. Mrs. James William McIntosh III. She did not realize at the time, that someday, she would want her own identity. The hope was that if she found the right man, her life would be great. When she found Jim, she fell in love with his self confidence. Here was a man who knew who he was, what he wanted and where he was going. She was "in love" with the notion that she could become him and they become *ONE*... just like the movies and just like Mother had promised.

Married But Not Happily

Jackie continued her story, "*I married Jim and watched him sell his way to the top. I dropped out of college and forgot my silly career dreams. I did secretarial work for the company and raised the children. And now, well, I have everything and I should be really happy. All the pictures look right. I have everything Mother said I would need to be happy... a big house, wonderful children, and a man who can do it all.*

But deep down inside of me, I don't feel good anymore. Sometimes I wonder if I am going crazy. When I am alone, I cry all the time. And when I am not crying, I am enraged. My rage scares me. I have never been so angry in my whole life. I am not sure who I am really angry at. At first I blamed Mother, because I realized that I married the man Mother had wanted to marry.

Then I get angry at Dad for not speaking up, and telling me to listen to my heart and my mind, or to Dad himself! Then I get angry at Jim. If you want to know what I really think, I'll tell you! I think that he isn't Prince Charming at all. I think he is arrogant and cocky, and I don't even think I <u>like</u> him. I am tired of being intimidated by him!

When Jackie finished her tale, I asked her when had she fallen out of love with Jim? She thought about this question for a long time before answering.

Jim's Story

Jim had his own version:

"She was cute, with her corny little glasses, she got great grades and bailed me out more than once. She'd type my term papers and sometimes even write them! She thought I was great. She didn't care if I got good grades. She knew I was

smart. She knew that I was a mover and a shaker, not a dreamer like her old man. I liked taking her places she had never been. She had been so sheltered. She liked my ideas and wanted to follow my dreams. She didn't seem to have any of her own... other than me. She told me I was her dream and that made me feel good. She was always laughing and smiling. I knew I could teach her lots, not book stuff, but life stuff. She'd spent enough time with her nose in the books. I'd show her other places... first of all the bedroom!"

Jim's account was very logical and simplistic. He was clear about what he wanted a wife to be. He was very honest about wanting someone who looked up to him and would follow his dreams. He wanted someone that wanted what he wanted, and would not get in his way. He admitted that he felt worldly and powerful around her, and saw her as really needing him. Otherwise, he rationalized that she'd have a pretty simple and boring life.

Jim presented a case of a man who needed approval and acceptance of his ideas and goals. He gravitated towards attention and recognition. He wanted feedback telling him that he was great.

And, Jackie, in the beginning, was eager to oblige.

Married But Also Not Happily

He continued his story.

"And then she changed, just like that! It's not my fault she changed... It was all those dumb books she started reading. All those self-help-woman's-do-your-own-thing books. Next thing I know she wants to go back to school.

I gave her too much... too much of an easy life. She started hanging out at the country club all day with all her little women friends. They would sit around and bad mouth men. Well I'm no shrink, but I know she hates her Dad. And now she hates me! I haven't done anything wrong. It's not my fault!

I haven't told her yet, but I'm leaving and taking the country club membership with me... besides, I've found someone that really thinks I am great. She's a little young, but what the hell, maybe I can train this one better. I deserve to be treated like I'm somebody, 'cause I am! I haven't done anything wrong. I admit that Mom was probably right all along. She never did like Jackie. But it wasn't my fault. I'll show Mom that I can find a better woman."

I asked Jim the same question that I had asked Jackie.

When had Jim fallen out of love with Jackie? As was his personality, he had all the answers and was quick to reply.

♥ KATHERINE AND KEN

Katherine's Story

Katherine described how she had fallen in love with Ken:

"He was an educated man, something no one in my family had ever aspired to. Everyone thought he was a good catch... and everyone was anxious to get me married off. I was just another mouth to feed... being one of eight kids and all. He was brilliant and had graduated from college with high honors. He was kind, but not outgoing and friendly. But I knew that he was just shy and that he needed someone to look after him, certainly not his Mother. She was so overbearing! He needed to get away from her and let me help him. She had made him almost helpless... I am sure she had dressed him every morning. But, not any more. After I took over, I took care of that and with much better taste I might add. I fixed him proper meals and kept his life tidy and organized. He would have been a mess without me."

Katherine, very stoical, relayed her story of why she had fallen in love with Ken. She described a righteous woman's account of finding a helpless and emotionally weak man who needed a strong woman. Since it was very obvious to her that he needed her, she felt loved. She loved this feeling and vowed to devote her life to helping him be a happier and a more outgoing person.

She had found someone who needed her! She had moved beyond hope and steered towards conviction. There was no doubt in her mind that she loved Ken, very much... and that was enough. She knew in his heart, he would someday realize just how valuable she was to him. All she had to do was be giving and patient.

She waited and waited and waited.

More of Katherine's Story

She continued her story.

"I wanted to believe that he loved me. I tried not to lose hope. However, to my amazement, I realized eventually, that he had shut me out. He devoted himself to his work and I think that he truly loved his work, but not me.

It was frustrating and difficult to feel needed when he was never home. His life had become his laboratory, sixteen hours a day. This infuriated me! He was NEVER home. I would call him, leave him lists, check up on him at the lab. I admit I questioned his every move. I tried to involve myself in my daughter's life... but, she rejected me as well. She was never home either... from the day she could drive a car. Next thing I know she has run off and eloped, eighteen years old! Can you imagine that!

My life is empty. Nobody needs me. It's just like when I was a child. Nobody loved me then, and nobody loves me now."

When did Katherine fall out of love with Ken? She shared with me that it was so long ago, she couldn't remember. After twenty-one years of marriage, she asked herself, had she really ever fallen in love with him in the first place? She thought she had, but she didn't know anymore. She didn't know anything. She concluded, that love was only a lot of pain and sacrifice.

Ken's Story

When I saw him, Ken had this report.

"Katherine was helpful. My father always liked her right from the beginning. My mother, on the surface, tried to be nice until things got serious. Then, it was obvious to all that she really resented Katherine. But, that was okay with me because I was sick of my mother always telling me what to

do. Mother had always been involved with me. In some ways, it was good because when the kids picked on me at school, she would be there to comfort me. But in some ways, I hated that.

I left college and accepted a prestigious and relatively important position with a large research laboratory, and went as far away from home as I could go. I was surprised at how lonely it was there. I didn't know anyone. It had always been hard for me to make friends. I went home when my grandfather died and there I met Katherine. She was somebody's niece. We were set up and were told that we would be perfect together.

Katherine was outgoing and instantly took charge. She was pretty, respectable and knew the right things to say and to do. I enjoyed her company and decided that she could make a good home for me. And anyway, it was time. I was 31 years old. And she was nice enough. I knew she would never leave me because she worried so much about if I had eaten, if my clothes were pressed, how much sleep I had gotten. And so we got married. I think we were in love."

Ken described a scenario of a man who had never developed social skills and who felt very isolated from the world of friends. He married thinking he "should" and that doing so would guarantee he wouldn't be alone. He was convinced that he couldn't do certain things very well.

More of Ken's Story

He continued, "*She says I'm a workaholic and she's probably right. She usually is. I work all the time. I still do, but, that is because I'm good at it. I have made lots of money. I get paid to have brains. And besides, Katherine bugs me when I'm at home. She is always nagging, and always has a list of jobs she wants me to do. She's always mad at me for something. I don't do anything right at home. I always set the glass on the wrong table. She's always wiping up. I just stay away. It's easier.*"

When did Ken fall out of love with Katherine? He had no idea. He had no idea what love was in the first place.

♥ ♥ ♥

♥   ♥   ♥

Falling

Out Of

Love

♥   ♥   ♥

If I Love You Enough
You Will Love Me
And Then If You Love Me
I Will Be Enough, At Last

But…

As I Love You More
I Love Me Less
And As I Love Me Less
There Is Less To Love

And It Isn't Enough At All

♥ ♥ ♥

*J*ackie and Jim, Katherine and Ken fell in love, got married and had every expectation of living happily ever after. They each fell in love and each fell out of love.

How? Why?

Jackie confessed that she fell out of love because she eventually decided that Jim was not a Prince after all. She began to see him as bossy, controlling and always needing to be right. She discovered that he did not know everything and that sometimes she knew something and saw things differently from him. She felt that this was never acceptable to Jim, and then she began to feel stifled and smothered. She had a mind of her own and it was coming into full bloom.

That was the beginning of the end.

Jackie needed an identity.

Jim fell out of love with Jackie when he decided that she was argumentative and critical of him. He told me that she liked his pay check, but recently, she was disrespectful and did not make him a priority. She would rather "hang out at the country club than run errands for him." He couldn't even get her to balance the checkbook for him anymore.

Jim needed approval.

Katherine stated that she had realized that she had fallen out of love with Ken because she could never get him to value her and all that she did for him. It frustrated her. He was either late for dinner each night or didn't come home at all. She wanted him to eat properly, and she thought it was her job to see that he did.

Katherine needed to be needed.

Ken shared that he fell out of love with Katherine when he realized that she was always bugging him... just like Mother. She wanted to know every minute where he was, who he was with and what time he would be home. He hated answering to her for every minute. It was easier to just lie rather than prove to her that he did have to work late. "No, she didn't have to keep dinner waiting... yes, pizza would be fine for him."

Ken needed security, and a guarantee of not being abandoned.

♥ *"Needs" For Love*

In both couples, the individuals fell in love based on an unhealthy need that he or she wanted to get filled. When the needs were filled, the partners no longer needed each other in the original way and deduced that they must be out of love. As their needs changed, and the partners found that their new needs were not getting met, they again deduced that they must have fallen out of love.

Jackie needed someone to depend on and to give her an identity. When she realized that she could begin to depend on herself and therefore, give herself her own identity, her partner looked unattractive.

Jim needed her approval, and when she stopped approving of him, he determined that he no longer loved her. Her need had shifted from dependency to independency. This was a threat to him, and he took her independence as a personal attack on his self-importance and worth.

Katherine needed desperately to be needed in order for her to feel worthy. And when Ken would not cooperate with this need of hers being met, she determined that she no longer loved him.

Ken's fear of being alone and abandoned sent mixed messages to Katherine. His inability to be intimate without being controlled caused much confusion. Ken agreed by default, he had fallen out of love.

As the relationships became enmeshed, involved and complicated with children, family and commitment, the couples became stuck, unhappy and searching for answers to make sense of their lives.

♥ *Rationalizations and Reasons For Staying*

Things weren't *THAT* bad... or were they? Didn't a person have to go with the flow, and give a little?

Wasn't marriage like that? There was no such thing as a perfect relationship anyway. Was there?

Wouldn't things get better when there was more money, or a bigger house, less work, or when the children were grown and gone?

Wasn't this just a phase that every couple went through? Wasn't it part of maturing and growing up?

Perhaps, a little affair or fling would perk things up. It wouldn't hurt anyone. Nobody would have to know. It would make it easier to come home. No one person could meet all of one's needs anyway. Variety was the spice of life!

And so the affairs began. Affairs of the mind, affairs of the heart, and affairs of the body.

♥ *Coping or Copping Out*

Jackie coped by going back to school and began an affair with her books. Jim coped by turning his attention onto other women, and had several affairs. Katherine coped by escaping through alcohol and had an affair with the bottle. Ken coped by becoming a workaholic and had an affair with money.

And so the lies began. Lies to each other and most of all lies to themselves. The withholding began. For the couples, the masked unhappiness and escaping via affairs became a way of life.

Whether we turn to sex, work, money, sports, drugs or alcohol, we numb what we can't fix, confront or change.

And we cope.

And we cop out.

But if only we were in love again... all would be better, wouldn't it? Love, the cureall. More specifically being *IN LOVE*, the cureall.

We blame a lot on love, and we give "in love" a lot of power. And yet we don't really know what it is. Even worse, we don't know that we don't know!

So what is it? What is falling in love and what does it mean?

♥ ♥ ♥

♥   ♥   ♥

What Love Is

And

What Love Is Not

♥   ♥   ♥

Falling In Love Is...

*F*alling in love is about hope. It is a secret wish that, "oh boy, all my needs will be met by someone else and I don't have to do it myself." It is about the relief that *FINALLY*, I will get the approval, the importance, the identity and recognition that I have never had, and that Mom and Dad didn't give me.

Falling in love is about the thrill of becoming whole by another person's presence. So, for example, if we are not very logical and organized, then we find someone who is, then we don't have to strengthen our weaknesses, our partners will "do it" or "be it" for us. Opposites attract and fall in love all the time.

And the very reason we fall in love with someone is often the exact reason we fall out of love with them.

Falling in love is about the excuse to not be responsible.

It is about expecting someone else to give you what you didn't get at home... the approval, the independence, the identity.

They Said
I Loved Too Much
The Truth Is
I Wasn't Loving Enough
And Some Of The "Love"
Wasn't Love At All

♥ ♥ ♥

Falling in love is about finding someone who wins the audition for the main lead of our own script. We all have pictures of the perfect partner. We know exactly what and how we want them to look, to dress, to be, and what to say, how to act... in order to meet our script. And when we find someone that looks just right, we think we are in love. And if they then act just right, we *KNOW* we are in love.

Falling in love is trying to be exactly who we think the other person wants us to be. We think we are perfect mind readers and we try to wear what we think they would want us to wear. We try to be talkative and profound when we think that they want us to be, and then we try to be quiet and demure when we think that's what they want. We are not only auditioning the other, but we are auditioning for the part in *THEIR* play as well.

Falling in love is a fix, a drug, a temporary rush and a high that always takes us up and always brings us down. It is an addiction. We know we shouldn't but we do it anyway. We panic if we think it is going away. We have intense cravings and withdrawals when we fall out of love. We act crazy and against our better judgement.

We are proud to be in love and ashamed not to be. We feel a sense of false pride when are in love, and a sense of failure and embarrassment when we are not.

Scott Peck, in *The Road Less Traveled* remarked that "falling in love was really only a lustful erotic experience". Well, we don't want to hear that! We swear it is not lust. We swear it is much more noble than just sex. We make a fool of ourselves and someone says it has to do with our sex urge! No way, we plea... it is more than that! Honest.. really, we plea to our friends. This is the real thing this time. We know it is. We feel it. Our hearts flutter and we can't think. It must be real... look what it has done. It has taken over our thinking!

Falling in love is about the rush and the hopes. Sometimes it becomes superstitious. For example, we don't want to say anything that might jinx it. It is a high that intoxicates our head into thinking our heart is really talking. The heart and the head are talking, and the head is telling the heart that "yes, yes, yes... this time, this love will last. This time we won't ever be abandoned. This time we will have the ultimate and proverbial approval. This time, this other person can make our dreams come true".

Our thinking is very twisted and backwards when it comes to the concept of "in love" and "out of love". It plays many tricks on us. And so we hang on. *IN LOVE* seduces us, tricks us, controls us and decides for us.

When I First Met You
I Knew That I Loved You
But...
That Wasn't Love At All

What I Loved Was That I Thought
You Were Everything
I Needed And Wanted

Now I Know That Loving You
Is Getting To Know You

♥   *In Love Tricks*

Jackie

Jackie fell in love with Jim, the first time she met him. We would call that love at first sight. Little did she know that love at first sight is just that... love.. at.. first... sight.   After she saw more, she did not feel love at all. She fell out of love with him when she got to know him and got to know herself.

Jackie had been tricked. It wasn't Jim's identity that she needed, it was her own.

She believed that she couldn't get her own identity when she was around him, nor her own power. She thought that he did not take her seriously. She believed as well that no one in her family had taken her seriously. When she would get angry as a little girl, they would think that she was cute and laugh at her. She felt like she had to be what Mom wanted her to be, and not her own person. No one encouraged her to follow her own strengths and ideas.

Jim

Jim fell in love with Jackie because he felt that she put him on a pedestal and thought that he was great. He needed and liked her reinforcement, to convince him that he was "good enough". He fell out of love with Jackie when he realized that she had a mind of her own. In his opinion, she seemed to never agree with him anymore, and she always had to be right and do it her way. She was always busy doing her own thing and this made him feel unimportant.

Jim had been tricked. Jackie did not idolize him at all. In fact, he thought that she hated him. What he did not know was that his true need was not to seek Jackie's approval, but rather to approve of himself.

Katherine

Katherine fell in love with Ken who she thought needed her. She, too, had been tricked. She did not know that what she needed was to approve of herself *and to value herself.* She fell out of love when he stopped coming home, when he wouldn't listen to her, and when she could no longer control him. When Ken was home, he would just shut her out by watching television or reading the newspaper. She hated it when he would continue to read the paper as she was talking to him. He didn't care about her she told herself, so she wasn't about to care about him. She couldn't get him to need her and therefore never felt that she was important to him. Well, according to her, nothing had changed. These were the same feelings that Katherine had experienced as a child when she felt no sense of importance in her family.

Ken

Ken was tricked into thinking that he needed Katherine and that somebody was better than nobody. He was tricked into believing that being alone meant that something was wrong with him and that he couldn't survive. He thought solving this meant love. Ken fell out of love with Katherine when he discovered that she drove him crazy with her nagging and controlling. He began to view her in the same way as his mother. He often wondered why women always wanted to run his life. Katherine didn't abandon him physically, but she did sexually. Ken thought that Katherine never wanted sex.   He, therefore, determined that she probably did not love him and he did not love her.

♥ *Good Kids Being Good Adults*

The couples were neither wrong, nor bad, nor cruel. They simply did what millions of other couples do to try and get their needs met. We look outside of ourselves for solutions. What we do, we have been taught to do; to be nice, not to hurt other people's feelings, and to do unto others so that the other will do unto us. We want to get from life what life has to give us. "Good kids" simply grow up to be "good adults".

Jackie and Jim, and Katherine and Ken learned the lessons well that Mother and Father had taught them.

So, what had Mother and Father taught them?

♥   ♥   ♥

Good Old

Mom

And

Dad

♥   ♥   ♥

J *ackie's mother* had taught her to find someone who would be strong and Jackie did this. She also learned that she needed a man to be strong and that she wasn't safe alone... nor was it good to be alone. As a child, she was smothered with protection. The beliefs were that males were protectors from life's hardships, and that a woman needed a man to keep her safe. Jackie's mother had taught her to act like a damsel in distress.

Jackie's Father

Jackie's father was always joking and being the clown. Every time she tried to talk to him about anything serious, he said, "ask your mother". Jackie really wanted him to talk to her, to tell her things and to ask her what she wanted to be when she grew up. But he never did. He told her not to study too much and not to worry. Someday, she would find a nice man to make her happy and give her children. When she would try to get him to talk to her about his feelings, he would say, "I'm fine. Go and play." But, she suspected that he wasn't fine, and this worried her. She knew that no one would listen to her, and since her suspicions were never confirmed, she learned not to trust her intuition and not to take her life seriously.

Jim's Mother

Jim's mother taught him that he was too cocky for his own good, to stop thinking of himself, and that he was basically a bad person because he was always showing off and trying to get attention. Deep down underneath Jim's cloak of self-confidence was a very insecure scared little boy who felt that he wasn't good enough.

Jim's Father

Jim's father, by description, was a real man's man. He hunted, fished and worked as a mechanic at his own garage. He knew what real men were all about and would teach his son. He taught Jim that men were superior and smart, and that women were inferior and dumb.

Katherine's Mother

Katherine's mother ran the show and expected Katherine to help her. Katherine was the only girl of seven brothers and Mother needed her help. Katherine was taught that women were supposed to look after men because men were clumsy, they spilled things and usually made a mess. Katherine's mother was constantly cleaning and Katherine cleaned too.

Katherine shared that she never felt like she got any attention and that she was valued because she was needed by her mother to help with chores, not necessarily because she was special. Being the middle child and the only girl in a family of 8, she had got lost in the shuffle and could only stand out for herself when she would bring home a stray cat or a hungry mangy dog.

Katherine's Father

Katherine's father went to work every day from 9 to 5. On the way home, he would stop off at the local pub and have his Jack Daniels. The whiskey dulled his nerves from having to face eight screaming kids and his old lady nagging at him. When he got home he would watch TV, eat dinner, and go to bed.

Katherine's father taught her that men were emotionally unavailable.

Ken's Mother

Ken's mother smothered him with guilt, protection, and love that always had strings attached. If he wasn't a good boy and didn't come home right after school, she would withhold her love and make him feel ashamed. Deep down he resented this, but had no one to talk to and no place to go. At school, the kids always made fun of him because he was so smart, and mother would always protect him and tell him it didn't matter because she loved him.

No one was good enough for her Kennie, and she made certain to not like anyone he brought home and to discourage anything that did not involve her. Ken was taught to love conditionally.

Ken's Father

Ken's father was a dandy, a runaround and a flirt with women. He was never home and when he did show up, he would smell of alcohol and go straight to sleep. There was something sneaky about him but Ken could never put his fingers on it. He would have nothing to do with his "patsy" son and had no control of changing the Mama's boy that his son had turned into.

Ken was taught that men are a mystery, and that women control things.

♥ ♥ ♥

♥   ♥   ♥

Twisted

And

Upside Down

♥   ♥   ♥

*T*he truth is that while we think we are marrying the one we love, we are really marrying the one who we think will give us another chance at getting what we need, and did not get in childhood.

In addition, we marry someone who is most familiar to us. Jackie married who she thought would fill her Daddy's shoes because what she wanted and didn't get was an active dad. Jim married someone who was warm and nurturing and looked up to him because what he wanted in childhood and did not get, was attention and adoration from his mother. Katherine married someone she thought needed her because she always wanted to be needed and feel important. And Ken married someone because he thought he should, so that he wouldn't have to be alone nor abandoned.

Furthermore, the truth is that Jackie married who her mother told her she should marry. Jim married someone who looked doting and dependent but had not yet spread her wings. Katherine married someone just like her dad who was never home and if he was, he was unavailable. And Ken married another mother, when what he really wanted was a dad to relate with.

♥ *The Wounded Child Marrying The Wounded Child*

Who had really married who?

♥ *Childhood needs that were not met*

When our parents do not love us in the way that we individually need to be loved, we do not grow into healthy and independent adults. Emotionally we remain injured children. When we choose our mate, our own inner wounded child meets another wounded child and "hopes" that he or she will fix or mend our wounds This creates children marrying children. The wounded child meets the wounded child, and thinks everything will be okay.

Is it any wonder that Jackie felt betrayed by Jim when she found out that he could not fix her identity? Or that Jim was betrayed when Jackie stopped approving of him. Or Katherine, when she discovered that Ken didn't want to be around her, and Ken, not having a clue at what was happening but just knowing that he felt lonely and abandoned again.

♥ *A little girl had really married a little boy.*

Whatever Needs We Did Not Get Met In
Childhood
We Try To Get Met In Our
Relationships

We Fall In Love With The Second
Chance

♥ ♥ ♥

♥ *Second Chance*

We marry who and what is most familiar to us, but what we seek is a second chance of getting what we didn't get in childhood.

Jackie married the Dad she didn't get and hoped she could have.

Jim married the Mom he didn't get, but wanted to have.

Katherine married a man just like Dad and hoped this time, she could get her needs met.

Ken married his mother not knowing what he wanted.

As a capricious thought, Jackie's father married Jim's mother and Katherine's father married Ken's mother.

♥ *Mirror, Mirror On The Wall*

When we see something in another that we dislike, it is mirroring for us something in ourself that we don't like. It is easy to see a trait in another, but not as easy to recognize it in ourself.

Jackie, as she grew older and came into her adulthood, began to despise the fact that her mother was so critical of her father, and yet Jackie was brutally critical of Jim, and so like it or not, what Jackie hated most she had become.

What We Dislike
In Another

We Dislike
Most In Ourself

She had become just like her mother. Jim (and Jackie for that matter) had it mixed up. Jackie didn't hate her father, she resented her mother.

Jim became critical of women, just as mother was critical of him.

Katherine became controlling, like her mother and conditional in her loving.

Ken resented his mother and grew to resent Katherine. He also was unaware of hate or love for his father, and therefore unaware of feelings for and about himself.

♥ *Roadblocks To Love*

There is no possible way of loving another until we love ourselves. We need to give ourself a second chance, and know, and say, and believe that we are *GOOD ENOUGH* already, exactly as we are.

There is no way to love ourself until we know, and understand, and accept ourself, exactly as we are.

We keep looking for love out there.

But love is not out there, love is inside. It is inside each and every one of us, and for some, it is very deeply buried.

♥   *You always fall in love with the person who needs from you what you have the most difficulty giving, but what you need to give in order to heal your own wounds.*

This concept comes from a magazine article that discusses Hendrick's relationship theory, Imago Therapy. This is a convoluted concept that unraveled, turns into a profound revelation. I wondered 3if this concept was true when applied to my clients. Let's examine our couples again.

Jackie

Jackie fell in love with Jim who needed her approval.

What was most difficult for her to give after awhile was approval of Jim.

However, this was what Jackie most needed to give in order to heal her own wounds. She needed to approve of Jim.

If Jackie could approve, i.e., accept Jim and let him be who and what he was without trying to change him, judge him and compete with him... she could then learn to let herself be who she was.

It would require however, that she stop judging her mother and detach from mother's needs and agenda.

*You Always Fall In Love With
The Person Who Needs From You What
You Have The Most Difficulty
Giving*

But...

*What You Need To Give
In Order To Heal Your Own Wounds*

(Hendrick)

Jim

Jim fell in love with Jackie who needed from him, encouragement to be her own person. What was most difficult for Jim was to let Jackie keep her own identity in the company of himself without feeling threatened. This is exactly what he most needed to allow in order to heal his own wounds.

He needed to see that her ideas and priorities had nothing to do with him or his importance. They were simply her ideas. He needed to stop comparing everything to himself and his needs, and let her be. If he could stop being threatened by her need for her own identity, he could heal himself as well.

This would require Jim's willingness to let go of the need for his mother's approval and begin to give approval to himself instead.

Katherine

Katherine fell in love with Ken who needed from her, unconditional love, which was most difficult for her to give.

She only knew how to love herself conditionally... the condition of being needed was her criteria for loving and valuing herself.

However, what she needed to give in order to heal her own inner wounds, was unconditional love.

Katherine's own need to be needed kept her loving conditionally. To heal, she had to need herself and to love herself unconditionally. This would require letting Mom and Dad's love go. She must understand their love as the best that they knew how to give, and that it had nothing to do with her worthiness as a human being.

Ken

Ken fell in love with Katherine who needed from him, what was most difficult for him to give, which was his need to be comfortable alone and not feel abandoned.

But what he most needed to give in order to heal his own wounds was to learn how to be alone and value Katherine, not out of neediness but value her for herself.

What is interesting is that we *ALWAYS* get our needs met, whether we are conscious of it or not.

Jackie ultimately became independent in the marriage and even more so by initiating the divorce. She also made Jim wrong and did not approve of him at all.

Jim made Jackie's approval of him insignificant by making her wrong and went and found another person to approve of him.

Katherine didn't get to feel needed, but she got to feel "right" about the fact that no one needed her. She was convinced that her need for being needed was legitimate.

Ken needed to get away and did so in his marriage by working. Yet, he also satisfied his fear of being alone by staying married.

♥ *Bumper Cars*

When Jackie's need for independence grew so strong as to bump into Jim's need for approval and sense of importance, they clashed. We could say their issues bumped into one another's.

When Katherine's need to control and to be needed bumped into Ken's confusing, distant feelings and actions regarding love... they clashed.

Each individual had his and her own way, to avoid the relationship and the seriousness of its deterioration. They each chalked it up to the fact, that well, the honeymoon was over. They settled for mediocrity, and low levels of expectations about how it is when one gets married. The willingness to accept staying together was a lesser evil than splitting apart.

After many years and many situations that provided "proof", Jackie and Jim, and Katherine and Ken decided that they really were not very happy and determined it must be because of their spouse. Each concluded that divorce was the only answer.

So what we have are four people who can prove that they are *RIGHT*, and can justify their feelings and their reasons for not being in love with the other person.

♥ *Escape Hatches Out of Love*

When we fall out of love we begin to escape the relationship. Escapes are excuses for not being with the relationship. Escapes allow us to not be intimate. We escape because we are scared; scared to admit that we married not from love at all, but rather from need and from hope. And then, when we feel wronged by the other person, we begin to exit. When we find that our needs are no longer being met, we escape.

So call it what you will, exits or escape hatches, the results are the same. We begin to pull away emotionally. Let's look at how each person pulled away.

Jackie began to escape intimacy with Jim by turning to her books and women friends. She said that she tried to talk to Jim, and it never worked, so she confided in friends. In reality, she confessed that she honestly enjoyed making him wrong.

She discovered that she had a mind of her own and for the first time, she was taking herself

Do You Want To Be
Right

Or

Do You Want To Be
Happy?

seriously, rather than believing in men as the answer, end all, know all. She escaped by over-committing in school, to her professors and college pursuits. There became no time to listen to some-one whom she had grown to not like. Jim escaped his intimacy with Jackie by flirting and taking other women to lunch. He escaped by seeking approval wherever his good looks would take him.

Katherine was very lonely and unhappy. She began to escape through liquor. She admitted that she found the martini lunches kept her happy at least temporarily. Then at night, she said that when she waited for Ken to show up for dinner, she drank wine. Often the entire bottle was gone by the time he arrived. She usually threw the empty bottle out and rationalized that he didn't need to know that she had drunk the whole thing. She knew that he wasn't much of a drinker, so he wouldn't ask for any.

Ken escaped into his laboratory and the seduction of making money. He admitted that business meetings were always very important and very pressing.. and "well, Katherine would have to understand." He acknowledged that his work paid the bills and gave her a great lifestyle. She didn't have to work, he rationalized. She seemed to always be shopping for a new dress for the latest fundraiser. "Charity work was good for her and she liked it. She didn't like sex, so let her donate her time. Maybe she would feel better about herself."

In marriages, we are often physically married, but emotionally divorced. When we divorce, we are often legally and physically divorced, but emotionally still married. As well, we often remarry the *same person* with a *different name*.

Why is this?

It is because we have not healed our childhood wounds, and we can't separate what we haven't healed.

- ♥ If we do not heal our childhood wounds...
- ♥ If we do not learn to meet our own needs...
- ♥ If we continue to seek out another relationship to meet our needs for us...

Then, we do not have a new relationship, but only a new face. We still use the same way of relating to the other person, which ultimately, yields the same end results.

♥ ♥ ♥

♥   ♥   ♥

Letters

From

Home

♥   ♥   ♥

My mom is my mom, is my mom
She always will be, always has been
and still is
So be it, and so it is.

My dad is my dad, is my dad
He always will be, always has been
and still is
So be it, and so it is.

♥ ♥ ♥

*T*o heal ourselves, it is critical that we heal our relationships with our parents. We must let them off the hook and *RE-PARENT* ourselves in the exact and particular way that we, and only we, know that we need. Our parents did the best that they could, given what they knew at the time and given their own childhood wounds. We must accept that premise and move on. Accept does not mean that we have to like, approve and/or condone how we were treated and loved.

We do not have to like our parents. It is okay. Liking has nothing to do with loving.

Healing means we must accept our parents exactly as they are, and let go.

What would be the value in hearing from our parents... all the things we secretly wanted to hear and to know, in *exactly* the way we wanted to hear them, and at the *exact* time?

Wouldn't it be great if our parents wrote us a letter explaining all the whys and unspoken reasons?

We Must Drop

Our Histories

Of

Mom And Dad

♥ ♥ ♥

♥ *From Jackie's Mother*

Dear Jackie,

I can only begin by apologizing. I tried to live my life through you and to give myself another chance. I married for the wrong reasons and wanted you to marry who I should have married. I was never able to love your daddy like I should. He was a wonderful man, but I wanted money and power. I had no confidence in myself because I was told that I was not very smart. I thought that if I had money, then I could cover up for not having brains. I wanted someone that looked good, not necessarily someone who was good. Your daddy was so good, not only to me but to the rest of the world. I could not appreciate that. I wanted to look good because I never thought I was good inside. I am so very sorry. I was also jealous of your intelligence. I smothered you and overprotected you and tried to keep you dependent. I told you that you needed a man, when you not only did not need a man, but you did not need me. That hurt. I wanted you to need me because that would have made me feel important. You needed your father and I sabotaged that relationship by always putting him down. When I pushed you into marrying "Mr. Wonderful", you left. I was devastated but I admit that I asked for it.

I told you to find a powerful man, and you did. However, you are the powerful one, my beautiful child. At times you are the mother and I am the child. Backwards I know. I ask for your forgiveness. I release you and set you free. Find your wings and fly.

Love,
Mother

♥ *From Jackie's Father*

My Dear Adorable Daughter Jacqueline,

Hello my child, this is your Daddy writing to you. It is time for me to speak up. I have been quiet all these years and have let your mother run the show because I lost confidence in myself. I also had to run the show when I was a kid with my five brothers and sisters, because my dad left us. I never got to be a kid myself, nor finish school because I felt sorry for my mother and all the mouths to feed. I guess I became burned out and bitter... not to mention the fact that I had no role model. I loved you in the best and only way that I could, which I know was not very active. Forgive me, for I failed you. Your mother was always disappointed in me, and I guess I loved her too much. I knew that I could never give her money like her dad did, and I always felt ashamed. At first I thought I could, but then I always ended up giving my paycheck to some hungry helpless down and out guy. Little did I know that I was the one that was down and out. You are a very intelligent child and I know that you always knew something was wrong with me, even though I lied, and said there wasn't anything wrong, and made a joke of it. You know, the old happy clown on the outside, and crying on the inside routine. Your intuitiveness terrified me. It actually made me become more withdrawn, but don't blame yourself, it is a great strength. Someday, it will serve you well. Be strong, follow your wildest dreams, get as many degrees as you wish. People will be afraid of your intellect. You will outgrow them and they will attack you. At times you will think that your are crazy, because people will not level with you, like me. *BUT YOU ARE NOT CRAZY.*

Love,
Daddy

♥ *From Jim's Mother*

Dear Jimmy,

Hello Son. Well, I have a confession to make. It is late in the game I know, but here it is anyway. Please forgive me for not loving you in the way that you needed to be loved. I did the best

I could. That is not an excuse just an explanation. For some reason, after you were born, I saw how much attention you got from everyone, from strangers, and from your father, because you were so handsome and so competent at everything you did. You were the model golden boy. I thought your good looks let you get away with too much and subconsciously, I decided to make sure to keep you humble. I didn't want life to come easy to you, because I rationalized you would take it for granted. I made a habit of putting you "in your place", criticizing you just to keep you honest and always telling you to not brag and not to boast. Nothing was ever good enough and that was only because I thought I should balance out the praise and accolades that your father was forever giving you.

I admit, I was jealous of your father's attention. After you were born, I felt like I did not exist. The sun rose and set on little Jimmy and the two of you were inseparable. From the beginning you preferred him and he let me know it. I felt incompetent as a mother because I could not satisfy you. As soon as Daddy got home you would stop crying. I was jealous and resentful... not only of the fact that Daddy satisfied you more, but that you took away Daddy's attention from me.

I want you to know that you are good enough, smart enough, handsome enough, and I approve of you exactly as you are. It is me that needs to have some interior work done. I compet-

ed with you and threatened you about you. You
are wonderful.

Love,
Your Humble Mother.

♥ *From Jim's Father*

Dear Son,

Boy oh boy... where do I begin? I see in
you all of my faults. I was really a macho kind of
guy... always needing to put women down. What
was really true was that I hated men! Imagine your
old man admitting that! I hated men because my
old man abandoned the family when I was nine
years old. My mother was so bitter and hated men
so much that I thought she probably hated me too,
since I was a male and all. I know it sounds ass-
backwards, but I felt I had to defend the entire
male population. I colluded a lot with you and got
you in my camp. I picked on your mother and
confided in you at the expense of her. It was
wrong. I browbeat her into thinking that men were
superior and women were inferior. She bought it
all right because her old man committed suicide and
she never got over it. Boy! What happened to all
the men in this family? Anyway, I turned into a
raging jerk and I don't want you to be one too.
You are great and so are the women in your life.

I know you have had an affair, well so have I, and it doesn't solve anything. Your mother, bless her heart, is a wonderful woman, and if she will forgive me, I will be good to her and other women for the rest of my life. I hope you can learn from my mistakes and stop looking for a weak woman to build you up. You are great and you don't need to put someone down to prove it.

Love,
Your Old Man

♥ *From Katherine's Mother*

Dearest Katherine,

Where do I begin? I never gave you any attention and this letter is as much for me as it is for you. I guess that means that I never gave myself any attention! I never let you be a kid, or put yourself first, nor be needy. I saw you as a comrade, even at four years old! Being the only girl in a family of all boys... I needed an ally. I couldn't bear for one more person to need me. I needed help desperately and didn't know how to ask. I just became the martyr and roped you into the role as well. I never had any time for you, nor did your father. When you finally did get married, I thought maybe your new life would give you a chance. Most of the boys had found themselves a "good woman" to take care of them, and so it was time for you to leave.

I guess I have to admit that I saw men as weak, helpless, and incompetent. I really don't have much respect for them and I always put them down. If they make money, I find fault with the fact that they can't cook. If they cook, I complain about everything and am never satisfied. I must be addicted to misery and crisis and terribly uncomfortable with calmness. Now that all of you are gone, I have no one to blame for my unhappiness. I have run out of fuel and no longer get pleasure from struggle.

I needed to be needed and boy did I create that! Eight children and a simple factory worker husband. I taught you to need to be needed and it is all wrong. All you need is to need yourself. You are beautiful, and worthy, and deserve to be pampered and admired and respected. You don't have to be needed by someone to be lovable. That is all backwards. And if no one needs you, then rejoice! It is okay. You are free! You only need to take care of yourself and learn to see yourself as a beautiful person. Fall in love with Katherine. Stop looking outside and dwell in your own heart... I love you... but, I want to tell you that for the first time... at seventy-nine years of age.... I love me. I accept my life and forgive me. I did the best that I could, and this letter is even better. It may be late, but still better late than never!

Love,

Mother

♥ *From Katherine's Father*

Dear Katherine,

Guess who... your Papa. I know you won't believe this but I am taking the time to write to you. I see you... I hear you... I notice you and I want to drop everything in my life and write you this letter. Nothing else matters right now, but you. Today you are my priority. I am cancelling everything else, mother, work, and the seven hungry acting brothers that demand all the time. But not now, this is for you.

I avoided giving you any attention for a couple of reasons. First, you acted like you didn't need any. Katherine could do everything... she could tie her shoes before everyone else, she could pour cereal in the bowl for her little brothers, she could run to the store and get bread and eggs, and not break a one. She could cope and manage on her own. We knew early on, that we didn't need to worry or fuss over Katherine. She never got into trouble, always did her homework and probably everyone else's too. Well guess what, we were wrong! We should have fussed over you. You did need something. You needed to be a little kid!

You needed attention. You needed to be treated as special.

But there is more. The other reason I avoided you, and this is really hard to say, was because I was afraid of your womanhood. You started to develop and I secretly was repulsed by my fear of being aroused sexually by my own daughter. I know that sounds sick, but I have learned that fathers struggle with this subconsciously or consciously, and heaven forbid, some act on it. I know my boundaries and I knew that I would never trespass my own daughter. But, if I am completely honest with you, I must tell you that the fear was there. It disgusted me and so I stuffed it and pushed you away. I know that one time, it was okay for you to sit on my lap, and the next time, as if overnight, it was not. I hid behind my paper, my Jack Daniels and my fatigue. Don't be like me Katherine. Don't hide and don't hide behind the mask of liquor to be close to me. If that is the only thing we have in common, what a tragedy. You are a beautiful woman. Stand tall and be proud of your womanhood. You are worthy of some wonderful man's attention and time. Bless you. Have and get everything you want, but from yourself first.

Love,
Papa

♥ *From Ken's Mother*

My Dear Little Kennie,

Dear, oh dear, oh dear... what have I done to you? Will you ever recover? Let me try to begin at the beginning. It was during the war and your father had gone. I had two miscarriages and the doctor warned me to not try again. But of course, I never listened to him, and finally carried that baby, a girl, to full term. She was born dead and I thought I would die with grief. I never talked about it, and for all I know I may still be grieving. Of course, I blamed myself.

Your father and I never really connected sexually. I was shy and inexperienced and afraid. He would get very frustrated at my ineptness and finally stopped trying. I was clumsy and inhibited. But more than anything in the world, I wanted a baby of my very own. So, you can see that when you were born and you actually lived, I was ecstatic. This is why I put all of my attention and energy into you. You became everything to me, my whole life and my, "emotional spouse". I pushed your father out of the bed... literally and figuratively, and never really let him back in. He naturally resented you and stayed away. I made him out to be the bad guy and convinced you that he didn't love you as much as I did... and to reject him. This was wrong and hurtful to you. It was hurtful to him as well, but I wanted to hurt him. I know that he began running around. He was very sexual and sensual... too much for me I guess... and I was intimidated. He was quite the romantic, and I always made fun of him in self defense, or nagged at him for spending the money on something so frivolous as roses at Valentine's day. You were my life. No one was good enough and everyone threatened my control and hold on you for myself. This was sick, I know now. I never taught you to cook, or wash your own clothes and convinced you that you needed mother to do it for you. Then you met that horrid woman, Katherine, who was about to take my place and did! I was devastated... and knew that then I would be left to face my relationship with your father, that I had sabotaged for years. So much had happened and we were so estranged. I never let you be with your father, because I was so angry at him, I did not want him to have the satisfaction of a relationship with his only son. Besides, I thought I needed to protect you from his dandy ways. Whenever you would reach out on your own, I secretly wanted you to fail so that you would realize that you really could not exist without me. Dear, dear, you grew to love me and to hate me. I know that you outwardly hated your father but inside you yearned for his love. I know that inside you hated me, but on the outside you acted as if you loved me and were indebted to me. Confusing isn't it? Well, it is no wonder you are confused. I twisted every emotional wire in the book. I taught you love in a warped, unhealthy way. None of what I taught you is correct. It is all twisted and backwards. I taught you manipulation and dependency and control and insecurity. Unlearn, Kenneth. Unlearn everything I taught you. Start again.

Love,
Mother

♥ *From Ken's Father*

Guess what! It is time for you and me to have a nice long chat. I have a lot to get off my chest. I left you, as well as your mother, many years ago. I left you because I couldn't bear the pain of loving a child and then having the child die. Your mother never thought that hurt me much because I hadn't carried the baby for nine months. But, I want you to know I was devastated. I cried quietly behind the booze, behind the women, behind the mask. I did everything I could to run away from the broken heart. When you were the only one who lived, I wanted to love you, but was so afraid, also you seemed so important to Mother and I seemed like such an interference. I hated myself so much for having affairs, that I really began to believe that I did not deserve the love from my son. I was a bum, a dandy and a drunk. The best thing I could do was to be out of your life. Little did I know that I had something positive to offer you, by just being the man in your life. You never did get a man in your life. You were brainwashed to see the world through the life of a woman... and a controlling one at that. I became afraid of my heart, because my heart always lead me to sex. My heart, I now know has nothing to do with sex. Womanizing has nothing to do with love. I didn't love myself, nor did I ever really love another, except for you. I wouldn't let myself. Crazy, isn't it... but true.

Love,
From Your Father

♥ ♥ ♥

♥   ♥   ♥

Loving

Yourself

♥   ♥   ♥

What If We Gave

What We Most Wanted?

♥ ♥ ♥

*H*earing what we always wanted to hear, knowing what we always wanted to know, and not just from anyone, but from the one that we want to hear it from, frees us. But, we don't get that, you may argue. We may never get that! Mom and Dad are gone, or unavailable, or wouldn't understand.

You are right. They may be gone, they may not "get it" for even if they are alive and do get it, they may never say it!

True. So what are you going to do? Hold out for the big day when they see the light? Hold out for the big miracle of them being different? No.

This is not about them. It is about you. It is about you becoming alive to your own needs and uniqueness. It is about getting *it* and giving *it* to your own wounded child, the child inside that keeps trying to get your attention.

It is not for a partner to fix. It is for you to fix. If you did not get approval, then begin approving of yourself. If you did not get attention, they begin by attending to yourself. If you were abandoned, then stop abandoning yourself.

If you needed to be needed, then rely on and need yourself.

Stop mistaking *NEED* for *LOVE*. Stop choosing partners because you need something from them and calling it love.

Well, if love isn't need, then what is it?

♥ *A Love Affair With Self*

Jackie became single, independent and earned her Ph.D. It felt good, she had an identity and independence. She shared this journal entry about herself with me.

"Hello self... how ya doin?"

"I'm really great, I answered... in fact, I am quite amazing... my ability to love is profound... to love myself that is... I am beginning to have deep pockets. I am okay really and truly. I am okay. I think I am having a love affair with myself. One from the heart... not the ego. I have just taken myself to a quiet little mountain town for the week-end, and rented a cottage. Me, myself, and I. I enjoyed the drive, top down, hair blowing, singing to the tunes of the Big Chill... 'I don't love nobody that don't love me, now... I don't need nobody that don't need me... I don't want nobody that don't want me.' We, (myself and I) bought a Sunday

paper, read it from front to back... laughed out loud at worldly absurdities, bought a great pair of winter boots and a red wool blanket. Ate a huge meal... without feeling guilty, left the restaurant, found a chair in the sun and took a morning nap. As the creek babbled by and the fall leaves fell and the sun passed in and out of the clouds, I discovered that I was good company to be with after all. Perhaps, on the drive home I'll stop and buy new linen napkins and a dripless candle, because "I'm coming to dinner." And maybe a pretty new nightie and put crisp, fresh sheets on the bed because "I'm going to bed with me..." And I'll keep fresh ground coffee and heavy cream in the refrigerator, and smoked oysters and brie, just in case I want to have a picnic..."

Jackie/Jacqueline

Jackie discovered that she did not need a man to make her happy or safe. That was Mom's belief. She found that her Dad was joking because that is how he coped. It had nothing to do with her. She could also let Jim be Jim. Jim was Jim. She could stop trying to make him wrong. She could accept him for exactly who he was and get off his case.

Jackie could accept herself, and that she didn't have to divorce Jim because he was having an affair. She could end the marriage because she in fact wanted to be alone to discover herself and all of her strengths and weaknesses. She needed time alone to heal, to mend and to take responsibility for her life decisions. She could love Jim for exactly who he was and let go. With dedication on her part and commitment to therapy, she sorted through what were her mother's beliefs and what were hers. She stopped looking for men who would speak up and speak out, and who were strong. She decided to speak up and to speak out, and to become strong herself. She could change her mind and experience the world differently. She had to learn how to trust herself, first and most of all. She took all the necessary steps to becoming whole. Not until she began to enter into a love affair with herself, could she freely love another.

In her journey, Jackie decided to do all of the traditional as well as avant garde approaches to learning and healing. This included psychic reading, group therapy and fire walks. She began calling herself Jacqueline, her given name. She found her identity and her independence.

Jim

Jim, and the Jim's of the world, usually do not seek nor stay in therapy for very long. As soon as it was evident that a divorce was on the rise, Jim chose to discontinue treatment. At one of the last sessions, he revealed that he did not need, nor want therapy, because he was getting remarried soon.

Katherine

Katherine decided that she really wanted a divorce and she wanted to be totally free to work on herself. She and Ken mutually agreed that it was time. She checked into an alcohol rehabilitation center and was very committed to working through her issues. She recognized that in order to do so, she had to become sober and alcohol free. As the haze of alcohol lifted, the clarity of the truth began to surface and become clear.

Ken

Ken decided it was time for a change. He'd had enough of his lab work and prestige and money. He began to invest in his own laboratory of self discovery. Where did his feelings come from anyway? And what was Love? He went into individual therapy, and got in touch with the concept of his own inner child. He joined a men's group and learned about male bonding. That was when he decided to call himself Kenneth. In individual therapy, he asked for more and more ways to learn. He learned about ages and stages of development, as well as feminine and masculine energy. He even signed up for a firewalk.

At the firewalk, he met Jacqueline.

Jacqueline and Kenneth

They were both in the process of healing and learning and loving themselves.

They found each other interesting and wanted to get to know each other better. It was not love at first sight nor were they even certain it was anything. Nothing felt familiar.

No bells went off.

She liked him.

He liked her.

That was all that they knew. And they liked spending time together.

A year later, they still liked each other and they still liked spending time together.

They began paving the way for a loving relationship. Would the romance come... or was it already present?

Romance was not the issue, nor the focus. They liked each other, and for now that was enough.

But wouldn't they get hurt, if they got "too involved?"

No Wonder
I Feel A Rush...

It's A Thrill Finding
My Perfect Partner

Forgive Me

Loving You Is
Discovering Who You Are

Not How You Meet My Needs

♥ ♥ ♥

Not if they remembered to give to each other because they wanted to, rather than to give because they had to, or in order to get something back.

♥ GIVING TO GET

The reason people get hurt in relationships is that they set themselves up. They manipulate the situation in order to get what they want. They give to get. Then when they don't get *it* they feel betrayed, let down, or annoyed. If we don't manipulate in the first place, there is no risk of being disappointed.

Likewise, if you give to yourself what you need, and what you did not get in childhood, i.e., approval and unconditional love, then you can allow yourself to give freely and without an agenda.

For many of us, this kind of loving is not familiar. It is possible that we may not recognize love even if it stared us in the face.

♥ ♥ ♥

♥   ♥   ♥

Relationship

Stages

♥   ♥   ♥

J UST FRIENDS

How many times have we been asked the question, "Are you interested in him?" And we have replied, "Oh heavens no, we are just friends. I can tell him anything. He always loves me, and accepts me, and is always there. But we are just friends. I wouldn't want to ruin it by getting romantic."

The term "getting romantic" actually means for many, "having sex."

Isn't it odd? When we go to bed with someone, everything changes.

Many so-called "romantic" relationships really mean that someone has slept with somebody, i.e., had sex with them. It has not necessarily been done from a loving relationship, but rather from a sexual drive. Understanding the difference between the sport of sex, and the purity of loving is crucial.

We often feel uneasy with our "lovers" in a so-called "relationship". We think that we have to "look good for" him or her, or we fear that we will say the wrong thing, look the wrong way, and fear that in the end they will leave us anyway. No trust. No security. And many conditions.

Think about it. We make love to someone we don't trust and can't relax around. And we don't want to make love to someone who knows us inside and out, and still chooses to be our friend.

♥ *ARE WE TWISTED*
    IN OUR THINKING AGAIN?

Jackie and Jim were definitely not the best of friends. Neither were Katherine and Ken. Jackie's best friends were her books and professors. Jim's best friend seemed to change with each affair. Katherine's best friend was the bottle. And Ken's best friend was his bank account.

What about chemistry! We argue that we cannot get turned on by our best friend. It would feel incestuous.

A part of "chemistry" is adrenalin. This adrenalin often comes from the rush, the high, and the hope, of finding something that we have spent a lifetime searching for.

If we become our own fix, and we are not looking for anything outside of ourselves, then we may not feel the rush when we meet someone. This is a good sign. I repeat, this is a good sign, not a bad sign. It says that we are coming from a place of choice, rather than hunger and need.

*If we become our own fix
and we are not looking for
anything outside of ourselves
then we may not feel the rush
when we meet someone.*

This is not necessarily a bad sign.

♥ ♥ ♥

But we argue, "I still cannot believe that my best friend is my perfect partner. Shouldn't I feel romantic?" Are we really asking to be turned on sexually, similar to a high that one gets from alcohol or drugs? Falling in love acts as a drug which is a *synthetic* turn-on. Synthetic turn-ons are time limited and usually last a short while. Then, the big crash and let down occurs. And as high up as we go, is as low down as we fall. On the other hand, a *natural high* is real and lasts forever. Natural highs become great memories.

♥ *RELATIONSHIP STAGES*

According to Gorsky and his *Intimacy Tape on Relationships*, there are four stages of a relationship.

- ♥ Superficial
- ♥ Companionship
- ♥ Friendship
- ♥ Romantic Love

Superficial is surface... on the outside. It is the relationship that we have with the waiter, gas station attendant or a one-night stand. Surprisingly, even after twenty years of marriage, couples still have a superficial relationship, a relationship strictly on the surface. Jackie had a superficial relationship with Jim and Jim had a superficial relationship with Jackie.

The second level is that of companionship, wanting company and not wanting to be alone. So if you call someone to go to the movie, and they say, "No, I don't want to go to the movie, I want to stay home," and you say, "Okay, I will call someone else." What you really want is some company. At times, Katherine and Ken were companions.

A friendship relationship would look quite different. The friend would ask you to go to the movies and you would reply, "No, I want to stay home," and the friend would say, "Well, I really don't care what we do, I want to be with you."

The fourth stage of a relationship is called romantic love. Because of the confusion around lovers and romance, I prefer to call it the stage when your best friend is your lover, and your lover is your best friend.

Romantic love is misleading. Some would say that being lovers is the ultimate and highest stage. However, we can be lovers at any of the stages.

Jackie and Jim were lovers, even up until the very end. Katherine and Ken started out as company, became lovers for a short time and never really reached the romantic stage. In fact, neither couple had experienced all four stages.

*Romantic Love
Is When*

*Your Best Friend Is
Your Lover*

*And Your Lover
Is Your Best Friend*

♥ ♥ ♥

Being romantic and being lovers are separate issues. We can have romantic friendships and never be lovers. We can be in romantic company and not be lovers. We can be superficial and be romantic. Conversely, all the stages can be interchanged. Progressing from superficial, to companionship, to friendship, and then engaging in a romantic lovers stage, insures a rich relationship.

We need to remember that the quality of the relationship is directly proportional to the quality of the relationship that each individual has with him or herself. This means that ultimately, we go through all of the stages with ourself.

Jackie began with a superficial relationship with herself. She grew to be good company and a friend to herself. Eventually, she literally fell in love... became loving to herself. And then, she could love another and let herself be loved in return.

Jim remained superficial with himself and with others. It appeared that he did not really like his own company and was not his own best friend. He talked a lot in therapy, about being great and thinking that he was wonderful. One has to wonder if he was trying to convince himself that he was okay.

Katherine had a long way to go, to get beyond superficial. She had to first be willing to look at herself, sober. It was painful, but she was eager and willing to go through the necessary treatment.

*Build the friendship
and the romance may follow*

*Build the romance
and friendship
may very likely not follow*

Ken went for it all! He decided to learn about himself, and was amazingly willing to take himself as seriously and as intensely as he had taken his laboratory work. He found the area of human behavior intriguing. He told me that I was the teacher and he was the student, and to teach him everything I knew. He wanted to know why he behaved a certain way, and why others behaved in other ways. His curiosity easily allowed him to explore his motivation, feelings, and actions. He grew to understand his issues of abandonment, and how he had in fact abandoned his own needs and feelings. He confronted his fear of being alone, and even found himself fiddling in the kitchen experimenting with a few gourmet dishes. He proudly announced mastering Cajun red snapper, boiled potatoes and broccoli. He became kinder to himself and his emotional needs, and truly began to like himself.

♥ ♥ ♥

♥   ♥   ♥

So What Is

Love Then?

♥   ♥   ♥

S o what is love then, if it is nothing that we thought it was?

To look at love and loving differently, we will look at different cases.

Love is different, and it has probably not happened to us before. That is why we don't recognize it.

Love is what feels odd, not what feels familiar.

Robin and Max

Consider Robin's account of "Just a Friend." *"Max is really a wonderful man. I can tell him anything. I love having him around. He is coming out to stay for the summer. No it is not romantic, we are just friends. I can't wait to see him. He flew 3,000 miles to stay with me after my accident and nursed me back to health. He got me to eat right, and back to running again."*

Robin described this scenario and was thoroughly convinced that there was nothing romantic to this relationship.

Little did she know that it was the most she had ever had from a relationship, and that the components of their relationship were the exact ingredients of a loving relationship. They had honesty, respect, openness and freedom.

Love is not knowing what will happen. And more importantly, not caring or being attached to what does or does not happen. However, being "in love" is thinking, hoping, and keeping your fingers crossed. Real love is not this at all.

♥ Love is a surprise.

♥ Love is innocent.

♥ Love has no agenda.

♥ Love just IS,

Robin and Max were loving. Did they get married and live happily ever after?

No. After many months, they decided to be sexual. Then, they together decided that they did not want to be sexual with one another. They did not feel "that way" about one another.

Did that jilt them? Hurt them? Abandon them? Embarrass them? Insult them?

*Be Willing
To Look Your Best Friend
In The Eye*

And Hold Their Hand

No, they were friends. They loved each other and then let go.

They will always have a mutually loving and respectful relationship. They know that each individual will never settle for anything less than what they had with each other, and that they will move forward and open to the next person that they choose and that chooses them.

They are safe. They are free. And they are loving. They are best friends. And best friends don't hurt one another by lies and betrayals. Friends also know that they are not responsible for another person's feelings and therefore, they do not fear or need to protect them from the truth. Friends also know that sexual feelings require the consent and congruence of both parties. It is a two-way street.

They had learned what they could from each other, and it was time to move on to the next lesson from the next teacher.

♥ Love does not require any effort, conniving, planning, manipulating, controlling or worrying.

♥ Love requires that you show up, be yourself, and see what happens.

♥ Love is thoughtless.

It Doesn't Really Matter

It's All Planned Out Ahead Of Time
Anyway

We Really Are Not In Charge
Of The Big Picture

All We Do Is Show Up

♥ ♥ ♥

♥ Love is slow.
  Layer upon layer.

♥ Love is not a rush.

♥ Love is a crawl.

♥ We look better and we don't know why.

♥ Love is a present feeling, not a past, nor
  a future.

When we "fall in love" it is a reminder of what we thought we never had, but always wanted to have in the future.

When we are "loving", we are surprised that it is even love at all.

♥   ♥   ♥

Loving

Stories

♥   ♥   ♥

"I Love You

And

I Am Leaving"

T *he Story of Tom and Rebecca*

Tom came into the office holding hands with Rebecca. They sat down very close to one another. They had struggled through two of her affairs and a serious operation. They had worked very hard in therapy to understand one another and their marriage. After clearing his throat many times, Tom began talking.

"You have been working with Rebecca and me off and on for the past year, and usually as you know, I am the last to talk. This time, I want to begin this session by telling you a story.

Once upon a time, there were two wolves who lived out in the forest all alone. One day the female wolf became ill. It was discovered that she had poison in her back leg. She limped along, but the male wolf stayed by her side every day protecting her from other scavengers and bringing her food. The male wolf decided to stay with her because she needed him. They never went very far in a day... always going at the pace of the injured female wolf.

In the beginning, they did not know if she would make it or not, and it was after many months before the female wolf began to heal. However, eventually she got better and friskier and wanted to roam. She wanted to go off on her own and explore new lands. She wanted to be free.

The male wolf had grown to love her very much and he had grown to want her for his very own. He had taken a lot of pride in nursing her back to health and in protecting her. He was torn between his needs and her needs. However, he knew that she needed to roam. He knew that she needed to find her own way and explore new territory. He knew that he had to let her go."

Tom then went on to say, *"Rebecca and I are getting a divorce."*

This is a loving experience. This 40 year-old man had rescued a 24 year-old woman from the emotional trauma she experienced regarding an abortion. He thought that he had done everything right by marrying her. Through therapy, they both grew to understand that she had had affairs because she was lonely and needed emotionally more than this self-sufficient man could give her. He had chosen to stand by her, forgive her, and tried to open up more emotionally about himself with her. But, it was difficult for him to share his feelings. When she had to have surgery, he stood beside her. He did so because he loved her. He had never considered his needs... nor given much attention to himself.

Of course, he didn't know that he needed to be needed, and that he thought that when she was well it might be his turn to do some of the things that he had wanted to do. She did not know that she had come into the relationship based on need. She was now 29 and wanted to spread her wings, and be free to experience life, in a healthy, open and honest way. She became interested in a career and wanted to stretch professionally.

She loved Tom and thought the world of him, and yet she loved herself too. She was beginning to think the world of herself as well, and wanted to go and taste it. She was willing to take responsibility for herself and honor her needs, and it had nothing to do with Tom.

Tom began to see that he had neglected himself. Being sent off to boarding school at a very young age, he had always learned to be self sufficient, and settle for emotional crumbs. Just a few crumbs. He could easily get by. He had mastered this years ago. Tom began to realize that he wanted more than crumbs. He wanted a shared, and mutual participating relationship.

This is a loving relationship. And yes, they divorced.

When we love someone, we let them go. We want for them what they want for themselves. We support them and their dreams, goals, ideas and needs.

But what about Tom? Was Rebecca loving Tom by staying with him? Was she giving him what he wanted and deserved? Was Tom asking and saying, I want this and I want that, and I want a woman to go to the places that I want to go?

What about the male wolf and where he wanted to go? Why had he been willing to go at a slower pace? He had been willing because he had roamed around long before she appeared on the scene, and what he wanted was companionship. He wanted to share his life with someone else. He had been alone and wanted to be with another to share in life. He thought he had found the perfect mate. It was perfect as long as she needed him, because then it guaranteed that she would stay.

When We Love Someone

We Let Them Go

"I have to let her go," Tom said. *"I love her that much."*

"And I have to go," she said. *"I love me that much."*

This couple did not have to make the other one wrong in order to justify their decision. They did not have to hate and get angry. Nor were they willing to be a victim, a martyr, or helpless. It was a brave decision.

♥ Loving is brave.

It was strange and yet there was something comforting in the decision. It was liberating to not have to hate. Tom knew that it had nothing to do with him. It was not about what he was or was not. It was about Rebecca and what she was, and what she wanted.

Only in loving herself enough could she not only set herself free, but, set Tom free as well. She wanted him to have someone who could and would love him, and who wanted to share a life with him. She loved him very much and she had to leave.

*If It Looks Like Love
It Probably Isn't*

*If It Doesn't Look Like Love
It Could Be*

♥ *Mary and Sam*

Mary and Sam are another couple. Consider their story. It is beautifully told in this love letter from Mary to Sam:

My Dearest Sam,

I feel you slipping from my mind. The miles apart distance my will. Not from any fault of yours, but rather from my choice to not put forth the effort to keep the fire burning. In fact, it is exactly what you feel like... a beautiful warm romantic fire that burned fervently crackling and hot. You felt so good, so comforting, so safe.

I am not nineteen anymore. I am not willing to keep running out in the storm for more wood. I have become lazy at love, at age 40. It is as if I want someone to tend it for me. Oh, I know you would. The problem is that it is not YOU that I want, or am willing to let... tend my fire.

I want to be known as an angel in your life, who came down and kissed your cheek, and reminded you of how special you are. I want very much for you to not settle for one iota less than the love and tenderness I gave you when I was willing to give. You are so deserving of breakfast being made for you, your back massaged, your eyelids kissed and on, and on, and on.

I want you to let go of me. I want to wander as I may. I want you to feel full that I came into your life, and not empty.

And you, you jolted my memory of how I want to be treated, and loved, and held, and touched.

You are beautiful Sam.

And I am going on.

Love me enough to understand.

Please feel joy because of me.

I do because of you.

And when we see each other again, which we will, I want to hug you and be still... capturing for that moment the thrill we have shared.

I want more... or different... or nothing... I am not sure. I just know that I love you, and it has nothing to do with my decision.

Lovingly from my heart,

Mary

♥ Love is a decision.

♥ We decide to love someone.

♥ ♥ ♥

♥   ♥   ♥

The

Path Of

Loving

♥   ♥   ♥

*Loving Is Encouraging Someone
To Be All That They Can Be*

*For Their Highest Good
Not Yours*

*T*he path of loving is a very different road than many of us know.

We must unlearn our assumptions about love in order to travel the path. Loving is a choice. Loving is a very slow process. Sometimes you do not even know that it is happening. Loving does not look the same or feel the same as what we've always thought was love. And often, it is not even recognized as love. Love slips in when you are least expecting it. That is the beauty of it. There is no effort.

♥   Loving is safe.

♥   Loving does not hurt.

♥   Loving is freeing.

♥   Loving is fun... it is light hearted and playful.

♥   Loving is easy... it is not work or effort.

♥ Loving is more... not less.

♥ Loving is being kind.

♥ Loving adds to us.

♥ Loving is open.

♥ Loving is honest.

♥ Loving is mutual respect and equality.

♥ Loving... is knowing that whatever issues come up for the other person, these issues have nothing to do with you. You are merely the facilitator, and the person's healing angel.

♥ Love is an honorable commitment.

♥ Love means you can say to the other person... "I have a problem with untidiness, and I need your help. Can we talk about this?"

♥ Loving is saying to a smoker, "I have a problem with someone smoking, can you, and will you help me find a way to manage this comfortably for both of us?"

♥   Loving is teamwork.

♥   Loving is win-win.

♥   Loving is allowing both people to meet their own needs and at the same time, honoring the other's.

♥   Loving has no fears.

♥   Loving knows no judgment.

♥   Loving is a feeling without an agenda.

There is no thought to what if, what next, what after. It is enough in and of itself, absent of expectation, absent of secret. It is an all absorbing, losing-track-of-time experience.

My Eyes Light Up And
I Am Purely Present
Purely Available And Purely Free

To Give
To Share
To Expose My Feeling, Myself
And My Soul

♥ ♥ ♥

♥ *HOW WELL DO YOU NOT GET ALONG?*

What happens when two people committed to each other butt heads with one another?

The strength of the relationship depends not upon how well the couple gets along, but rather *how well they do not get along.*

It is easy when it is easy. The challenge is to make it easy when it is difficult.

Cathy and Bill

Cathy and Bill had been in therapy and had completed a lot of work. However, every now and then, they would get stuck. They were angry and presented this scenario.

Cathy, trying to be calm, blurted out, *"I realize that I am taking everything Bill says personally, but it is personal!"*

Bill interrupted and said, *"It is not! When you act like this I have no choice but to leave you alone!"*

Cathy interrupts, *"Well, when you pull away and withdraw, I take it personally!"*

Already, they had forgotten a few basic rules of communicating which are:

♥ Not to interrupt
♥ Not to defend

♥   Not to blame

However, when we are in an "upset mode", we can forget.

Which came first, the "taking it personally" or "the withdrawing"? It doesn't really matter. When we are committed to a loving relationship, we need to lose interest in who is right and who is wrong. We must strive for and focus on understanding. All that is important is that each party know themselves well enough to know what their buttons are, if they are being pushed, and what to do about it. Cathy knows that she usually takes things personally. And for Bill, when things get tense, he always withdraws. They know this and they can usually identify it when it occurs.

♥ *ASLEEP, AN UNCONSCIOUS WAY OF LOVING*

Loving in an Unconscious Way is:

♥   Buttons get pushed

♥   Blaming

♥   Building a case

♥   Blowing Up!

Loving the old way is a circular process that only leads to the other person doing it back to you.

♥ *AWAKE, A CONSCIOUS WAY OF LOVING*

Loving in a Conscious Way requires a new way of relating to one another with absolute love and support from heart to heart.

We can...

- ♥ Be aware that our buttons are being pushed and say thank you, understanding that this is an opportunity to grow and heal, once again, and to get rid of an old childhood wound.

- ♥ Replace the pronouns of you with I, and take responsibility.

- ♥ Build a bridge of understanding and share from a place of love.

- ♥ Experience the natural high, that understanding and being understood brings.

Cathy and Bill decide to try to understand what's happening, rather than blame one another. They both take a deep breath and try again.

Cathy says, *"Bill... I notice that I am feeling really personally attacked when you withdraw, and I don't want to feel this way towards you, or because of you. Can we talk?"*

"Yeah, you are right," Bill said. *"I admit I am withdrawing and go back into my survival posture."*

Cathy continues, *"When you come home from work and you have had a bad day, I resent having to quiz you to find out if it is something that I have done or if it is indeed involved with work."*

"Well, when I have had a bad day, I resent walking in the door and answering your questions about if it is you or not." Bill said.

♥ THE TECHNIQUE

I, then, reminded the couple of the technique to use when trying to understand and listen to the other. The technique is to:

♥   Repeat
♥   Check It Out
♥   Relate

Cathy says she feels resentful of having to quiz Bill.

You Have To Be Willing

To Show Up For The

Conversation

Bill then repeats back to her what he thinks he heard her say, and then, checks it out with her to see if that is correct.

"So, I hear that you resent having to quiz me and that you feel like you have to quiz me because I am not offering any information."

He thinks for a minute and recalls a time when he had to squeeze information out of an uptight boss, and remembers that it feels degrading. *"Yes, I can relate to that feeling Cathy"*

Cathy feels grateful and says, *"Thanks, Bill, that means a lot."*

This progress in communication encourages her.

She wants to return the gift. *"And Bill"*, she repeats, *"What I heard you say, is that the last thing you need when you walk in the door is to be interrogated by me, and you really aren't in the mood to care about my needs at that moment. So then,"* she checks out, *"you have to choose between meeting your needs, which is to take a break... or attend to one more person pulling on you, is that right?"*

♥ *LOVE IS MELTING*

He melts. *"Yeah, you got it Cathy."*

What Did You

Hear Me Say?

♥ ♥ ♥

Cathy thinks for a moment and relates. *"That is how I used to feel every day at my old job and that's why I quit! I felt like an octopus being pulled in eight different directions!"*

Bill is relieved, *"Yeah, that's right... thank you, Cathy."*

Now, we have not found a solution to the problem of Bill unwinding from a hard day at the office. However, we have created a loving environment by repeating, checking out and relating with the other person's perspective.

Sometimes this is enough... just being heard.

Cathy does not have to fix Bill's withdrawing, and Bill does not need to fix Cathy's insecurity about thinking that she did something wrong.

♥ *THIS HAS NOTHING TO DO WITH YOU*

Cathy needs to use this as an opportunity to reinforce that Bill's behavior has nothing to do with her, and that it is Bill's issue. What she is feeling is an old feeling, or her inner child rearing its head. Cathy needs to go to her own inner child and say to her, *"You are fine, you have done nothing wrong, this has nothing to do with you, you are safe."*

Bill needs to go to his wounded inner child and say, *"Look Billy, you don't have to hide and withdraw. This person is safe for you to talk to, she is your friend. She is not your mother. She's not going to criticize, and she will give you the space you need to calm down, just ask."*

Loving means being there to support the other person while they process their own issues, and at the same time, processing your own.

After we have been heard, and the laundry is sorted out, meaning that we know whose issues belong to whom, we are ready to ask the other person what do they need?

Cathy says to Bill, *"I need you to tell me if it was rough at the office today, and that this has nothing to do with me, and that, you need thirty minutes to yourself to unwind."*

Cathy needs to realize and tell Bill that she has been home for an hour before he arrives, and that she is anxious and eager to be chatty with him. She can tell him that she now understands and will wait 30 more minutes. Furthermore, she does not want her eagerness ruined, nor does she want to feel disappointed and shut out.

He understands now, that surely she would feel disappointed after waiting, and that he does not want to be disappointing to her.

♥   They have connected.

♥   They have communicated.

♥   They have understood each other.

They have grown and made a deposit in the bank account called, you and me, called *US*. They are free to spend an intimate evening in a loving and gentle manner.

♥ ♥ ♥

♥   ♥   ♥

More

Paths of

Loving

♥   ♥   ♥

s mentioned earlier, blame is always off track. When we find ourselves blaming, we know that our buttons have been pushed.

When buttons are pushed by someone else, resist the temptation to blame, and use it as an opportunity to see something about yourself. It takes practice and patience to see progress in being loving in a conscious way.

Here is a Button-Pushing scenario.

♥ *BUTTONS PUSHED*

Consider the following letter from Suzanne to Paul written after an argument in which both partners left angry.

My Dearest Paul,

"I really wanted to blame you. I wanted to judge you and feel sorry for myself. Without much trouble, I began remembering all the other times you behaved this way, and I began building my case.

After I built my case strong and clear, and of course I was absolutely correct, I lowered the boom. I could easily say to you that you drink too much when you are away, and why can't you ever stay in the hotel room by yourself.
And why do you always have to have company around you! (As I write this, I see how ridiculous this sounds, but it was a very strong and true feeling at the time).

Once I got going with this line of reasoning, the ego jumped in, front and center and took over. The ego began to scream in my ear and argue; "those are facts, this is not an opportunity for me to grow or to look at myself, this is clearly your issue, and I say you drink too much. This time, buster, this is your problem". My buttons had been pushed.

I really wanted to blast you and felt a twisted sense of satisfaction in being right.

♥ *AND THEN I REMEMBERED AND WOKE UP*

The Poem:

> *YOU pressured me.*
> *I pressured me to be all the things I thought*
> *I had to be for you.*
>
> *YOU walked all over me and used me.*
> *I allowed myself to be walked on and used*
> *you as an excuse.*
>
> *YOU lied to me.*
> *I lied to me about you.*
>
> *YOU put me last.*
> *I put myself last when I was around you.*
>
> *YOU were so rigid.*
> *I was so rigid about who it was that I want-*
> *ed you to be for me.*
>
> *YOU thought you were perfect.*
> *I thought I was perfect in my assessment of*
> *how things should be.*
>
> *YOU said all the right things.*
> *I heard all the things I wanted you to say.*

YOU confused me.
I confused me in order not to see the things
I did not want to see.

YOU were so self-centered.
I centered myself around you.

YOU were afraid to let yourself love.
I was afraid to let myself be loved.

YOU were afraid to commit to a relation-
ship.
I was afraid to commit to myself.

YOU acted like you really loved me when
you were around me, and then you left me,
and you changed.
I acted like I was really loved when I was
around you and when I was left, I changed.

YOU were not trustworthy.
I did not trust my worth.

YOU only wanted me when you were
lonely.
I was so lonely, I only wanted to be wanted.

YOU didn't really love me.
I didn't really love me.

YOU mirror for me what I most need to see.

Thank you for all that you taught me.
Now I can see.
Now I am free.

I remembered the trickiness of the ego. I remembered that I had committed to absolute respect for the source of who each of us is. And I remembered I had to drop blame, drop criticism, drop judgement, drop comparison, and very importantly drop history.

I remembered and chose to step through it, and rise above this way of looking at the problem.

I remembered I wanted to choose love, loving, and lovingness. I remembered that it was quicker to blame, not necessarily easier, but quicker to point the finger. I remembered that I did not have to rush through this, and that I could go slow, and as I pointed that one finger at you, I remembered that there were three more fingers pointing back at me.

I also remember that with metaphysical laws, they don't just apply when it is convenient, they apply all the time and to all situations.

I remembered that I had to rant and rave, get it out in the open, get it off of my chest and get on with it.

I took a deep breath.

I looked at what was being mirrored for me, and I replaced the pronoun you with the pronoun I.

So I replayed the scenario in a loving manner. The truth of the matter was this. This is what was actually going on that night when I spoke to you on the phone. I had decided that it annoyed me that you had been drinking too much and staying out too late with all "those people".

In mirroring the situation for me, I remembered that I always worry about my drinking, if I have had too much to drink. I am always critical of how much, when, and with whom I am drinking.

Also, I always want to be alone, and I have to work at being with someone who loves me.

By putting my energy into making you wrong, I could avoid looking at myself. The truth is that I am ready to stop beating myself up for having a good time, and for taking time for myself to relax. I do not drink too much, and I make much too big of a deal about a glass of wine.

And it is also time for me to learn to be with someone that loves me, and that I feel loving towards. I have mastered being alone, and now I need to be relaxed and free in the company of another.

I was ready to share with you what I had experienced, and to literally thank you. I could now come to you from a total space of loving, and open my heart to you.

I could feel close, and I could evolve to the higher place where I want to be.

This all gave me a rush... and a total sense of pure love. Pure love is a big place and fills the heart with joy. It is the natural high that we can give ourself when we stretch and commit to being loving.

Lovingly,

Suzanne

♥   ♥   ♥

The Only Commitment

Is To

Ourself

♥   ♥   ♥

*Today Was A Struggle
That Is Not Loving*

I Must Have Been In The Way

*T*he only commitment one needs to make, is to one's self. If we commit to being loving then the worry and struggle is over.

Loving is like a golf swing. With a golf swing, one has to get out of the way of the club and let the club swing through and hit the ball. So, to with loving. We must get out of the way, and quit trying to manipulate the situation and let the chips fall as they may.

♥ *Let go and trust that the perfect partner is already in front you... there is nothing to do.*

However, before we can see the perfect partner, we must be able to see ourself. If we commit to ourself and have a loving relationship with ourself, then the rest will take care of itself.

*"One who is free to be poor
can enjoy money.*

> *One who is free to be sick*
> *can enjoy health and well being.*

> *One who is free to be alone*
> *can enjoy a partner.*

> *One who is free to die*
> *can enjoy living"*

Author Unknown

We must be willing to let go of our attachment to finding a partner and focus on finding ourselves.

♥ *MELANIE'S STORY*

Melanie had let go and committed to being loving to herself. Melanie insightfully described her story as follows:

"I've done my homework. I have worked at healing my wounds and dealt with my parents. I have ended a very dysfunctional relationship and I know well my pattern with men.
I realize that I have not been involved in loving relationships. I've been involved in cat and mouse games of winners and losers: chase games - called control.

I call this way of relating "teenage", because when I get around potential "dates" I feel like a giddy high school girl.

I know that my old way was to meet someone and latch on to him as if he existed on this planet so that I could survive. I easily remember the panic when he wants to leave and the feeling of devastation inside. I know I am very dramatic. I say things like, "I can't live without him!" I act crazy, I feel crushed and broken hearted. I think I'll NEVER get over him and that there will NEVER be another.

Then I vow to never love again!"

But of course, the vow to never love again does not last, because Melanie, like the rest of us, truly wants a relationship. Likewise, none of us want the kind that hurt.

Guess what! This is good news! There does not have to be another dysfunctional relationship in your life ever again! The relationships that hurt are not loving.

♥ WE ATTRACT WHAT WE ARE

There are many men and many women who have healed their wounds, done their homework and truly are open to having a new and different relationship in their lives. We don't meet them

He Wants Me
But I Don't Want Him
I Want You
But You Don't Want Me
You Want Her
But She Doesn't Want You
She Wants That Other Man

♥ ♥ ♥

if we are not like them. We always attract what we are, and so if we are dysfunctional in our way of relating to another, then we will continue to attract dysfunctional partners.

As Melanie healed and grew, she found that there were many others who were at the same place that she was, and at the same time in their awareness. Melanie had a history of attracting men that were not available; the non-committing type. That was because as we discussed, she was non-committing herself. Her fears of commitment and intimacy were classic.

- ♥ The fear of losing her identity when she got into a relationship.
- ♥ The fear of too much being asked of her.
- ♥ The fear of abandonment.

The ego slipped in:
"But how can you be certain that you won't foul up?"
"No," she said back to her ego, "I cannot foul up, because every relationship is perfect."

Melanie shared that she had to refresh her mind by remembering to commit to staying herself and not losing her identity. She was willing and determined to say *no* when she wanted to and to not say *yes* just to please or impress. In addition,

*My misery dresses me
as my soul sneaks a peak
at my richness and wealth of God's day.*

*God's day is great.
My day sucks...
The years click by and still I am alone."*

♥ ♥ ♥

she was committed to not abandoning the relationship if it got sticky or *too intimate*.

She remembered to give up *assumptions*, and committed to getting to know her partner, and accept him for who he was, rather than who she wanted him to be. She knew to not audition men anymore. She remembered to not blame the other person and to take responsibility.

And finally, she remembered that the quality of the relationship was only as good as the quality of the relationship that she had with herself. Yes, she knew that she loved herself very much. Yes, she could love and be loved by another person as well.

Melanie was still alone, and shared that she did not want to be alone any longer.

♥ THE TRUTH BEGINS WHEN YOUR BLUFF GETS CALLED

Melanie said that she wanted a loving relationship and shortly thereafter, she attracted not one but two men who wanted a relationship as well.

*Once We Have Made
The Commitment To Ourselves
That We Want A Relationship*

*It Is Only A Matter Of
Choosing Which Partner
We Want To Commit To*

♥ ♥ ♥

♥ *AGAIN, WE ALWAYS ATTRACT WHAT WE ARE*

She met Jesse and they connected instantly. They talked, related and shared their past relationship experiences. He owned the fact that he had a major commitment problem. He was forty years old and had never been married but had been in therapy, and was bound and determined to approach a relationship differently this time. He usually would rush right into the relationship, which often meant, rush right into bed with the woman. This time, he wanted to get to know the woman first, and go very slow. For awhile, this felt safe to Melanie. But, after a couple of months, she wanted more time with him and a deeper level of interacting. She wanted to "speed it up" a bit.

Then, there was Richard. Melanie shared this account.

"Richard is great! He knows what he wants and he wants to get right into it! He is ready to commit to a loving relationship. He is tired of dating and being superficial and he is willing to lay all his cards on the table. He wants to spend as much time as his work permits to get to know me. He is happy, open, and honest."

Melanie liked them both very much. As time passed she said that she felt very loving towards each of them.

*It Doesn't Matter
Who We Are Attracted To*

*It Matters Who
We Choose*

Richard knew about Jesse and Jesse knew about Richard. No one had slept with anyone.

She went on to describe her story.

"One weekend, back to back, I heard myself say to Jesse... Speed up! And to Richard... Slow down!"

Well, which is it? Do I want to speed up or slow down? Or if I am honest with myself, am I trying to manipulate again? Do I want to get the slow one to speed up, and the fast one to slow down? Am I loving or am I controlling?

One day, much to her surprise, Jesse in essence said, *"Okay... let's speed up. I love you. I want to commit to you and here I am."*

Melanie went into a momentary tail spin. *"Oh my God! Do I really want that?"*

Conversely, of course, as timing would have it, Richard had decided to slow down and told her so.

"Oh dear, do I want that? What would happen if I told Richard that I had changed my mind? I want him to be just like he is and I am going to commit to him."

Would Richard be as eager to love her?

*When We Ask For Something
And Then We Get It*

*We Get To Find Out
If We Really Want It Or Not*

Jesse called her bluff.

And she called Richard's bluff.

The real question is not if he or she is the "one". The real question is do you want to engage in a loving relationship with anyone? Or do you just play games of conquer and conquest?

It doesn't matter *WHO* you choose. It only matters *THAT YOU* choose, and that who you choose, chooses you too.

When your bluff gets called, you get to find out what and who you truly want.

Melanie made a choice.

And got to find out.

♥   ♥   ♥

Conscious

Partners

♥   ♥   ♥

C ONSCIOUS PARTNERS COME FROM A SPIRITUAL SPACE

There is no room for the ego in conscious and loving partnerships. There is no room for right and wrong. There is no room for grudges and blame.

There is only room for acceptance, forgiveness and understanding.

We don't need insurance and guarantees from our partners, because there is nothing to guarantee. There is no fear and no hurt. Yes, sometimes there is sadness and disappointment, just as there is joy and thrill. There are also no hidden agendas and secrets. *WE* don't exit the relationship when it gets tough, we face it, and we show up for the conversation. We do not judge. We understand the rules and the rules are out in the open. The rules are few. Honesty, openness and acceptance.

Conscious partnerships are here to stay. We want them. And we can have them. They are the purest form of intimacy.

Where do we begin, now that we are recovered? Where do we begin now that we are independent? How do we couple, together, as individuals?

♥ *COURTING*

Remember that word? Courting. That is where we begin. We need to court one another. Like we do when we first meet someone. We are kind, considerate, and gentle. We share what we have because we want to and we listen to the other with an open mind. We are interested in getting to know them without preconceived opinions and mindsets. That is the fun of meeting someone new. The fun wears off when we think that we already know everything that there is to know about the person. Then, we tune out and stop listening. Courting means we wash our hands and face before we meet someone and pay them respect and common courtesy. We give our partner a chance to speak up and speak out.

We go slow and we get to know them. We see them in as many situations as we can... at work, at play, alone, with our friends, with their friends. We also pay attention to how they treat the people in their past. Someday, that could be us. We dress up and we dress down. We do it all and we watch. And all before, and in lieu, of being sexual.

In conscious relationships, we show our cards as quickly as we can. We lay out our dreams, our wishes and our plans. We tell and share the truth of who we are and what we want, right up front.

But, you argue, that might scare someone away! Then, so be it. If they run early in the relationship, chances are high that they would have run later.

If we want a committed and fulfilling relationship, we say that we are interested in getting to know someone for the purpose of finding out if there is any potential. If we are only interested in dating and not having a committed relationship, then we say that. It doesn't really matter what we say. It only matters that we say it, honestly. The real you will flush out eventually, whether it is now or in ten years. Being open and honest with yourself from the very beginning ensures that both you and your partner know who you are and where you are coming from.

With your existing partner or a different one, we begin again by returning to courting. We begin as if we know *NOTHING* about the other person. Chances are, we really don't know anything. We only assume.

Whatever we do during the first few weeks of a relationship, determines the rules of the relationship years down the road.

If we are a woman who likes to have our car door opened then we sit in the car until that hap-

What If We Spoke
What We Most Withheld

And We Were Still Liked?

♥ ♥ ♥

pens, or we ask that of our partner, then our partner will open the door. If we would like that to happen, but we are afraid to ask, or we hope that someday the door will be opened, we are barking up the wrong tree, called the tree of mind reading. If we try to impress someone with what we think they want us to be, we miss the opportunity to be who we are. We must not be afraid to be ourself. We must ask for and share what we like and do not like... right away.

♥ *IN LIKE*

One of the surest signs of a working relationship is when one partner says about the other partner, "I really like him or her."

When I ask married couples if they're friends and they say "no, not really", I know we have trouble.

Liking someone has been underestimated... being madly in love with them has been overrated.

Liking someone requires time. It takes time to get to know and to respect someone. If you respect them, that respect will insist that you treat them kindly and fairly.

When the respect is gone, the relationship is gone.

♥ *DO IT DIFFERENTLY*

If what you have been doing in relationships has not yielded a healthy relationship, then consider doing it differently. Treat your partner as you would your friend.

Do not be afraid of ultimatums. Simply learn how to speak to your partner in a fair way, in a way of ownership. For example, "I am interested only in a monogamous relationship with you. If that suits you then we can continue. If that does- n't, we have to discuss it. Monogamy is important to me and it is important that I honor that."

"Be committed to the partnership regardless of the person."

Remember that the partnership is the "con- struct" of the business. Just as you would not walk from a lucrative, high potential business, so too, it must be in a partnership with another person.

- ♥ Throw out the old pictures of marriage.
- ♥ Throw out the old roles of husband and wife.
- ♥ Recreate new pictures.
- ♥ Rewrite the roles and the rules.
- ♥ Adopt a new language.

*Liking Someone Has Been
Underestimated*

*Being Madly In Love With Them
Has Been Overrated*

♥ ♥ ♥

- ♥   Don't be so quick to tell someone you love them. Wait until you have mastered liking them.
- ♥   Be engaged in the partnership.
- ♥   Be "in marriage", not married.
- ♥   Be In Loving, not in love.

Then and only then, discuss being sexual. Discuss what that means to you. What will the rules be? Will you date others at the same time, but not sleep with them? What will the expectations be if and when you become sexual with one another.

A partnership is a two-way street. Do not do all the work! Learn how to share responsibility of the relationship with your partner.

♥   *Terry's Story*

Terry called in a panic. *"I know what loving is. I have been practicing what I learned, but right now I feel swept off my feet and so I have told him I cannot see him any more. It is a long distance relationship and every other weekend was fine for awhile, but now I want more and I don't think he can be here much more and I cannot go there. I can't demand that David move here, because what if it doesn't work out! Then it will be my fault for asking him to move!"*

Be Committed To The Partnership
Regardless
Of The Person

Whoa! Whoa! Whoa! Slow down.

Terry does not have to do all the work in this situation. It is not for her to figure out how and if David can see her more often. It is her job to tell him how much she cares and what she can do and what she cannot do. Then, it is for her to give the situation to David and let him participate in the decisions and choices that he can and will make.

A replay of this would be:

"I really like you David. I want to see more of you. And I need to know if you feel the same way and what you want to do about it."

After a first phase of courting and dating, every couple hits another plateau or second phase. It usually hits about the second or third month. The relationship either ends, hits the wall, or climbs over to new territory.

♥ *HURTFUL HINTS*

At the second phase, we usually begin to hear hurtful hints. David says to Terry, "You should probably marry that rich guy you were telling me about before you met me. I can't afford you."

What she thinks she hears is that he thinks that she is materialistic.

What I hear as a trained listener is that he is checking out the water to see if he should continue to pursue the relationship or back out.

When we try to protect our egos from being rejected, we get defensive and evasive. We become afraid and don't really say what we mean and we hope the other person will get the "hint". In conscious and loving relationships, we don't hint. We say what we mean. We take out the guessing and lay all cards on the table.

♥ *THE GIFT OF RECEIVING*

What's Love Got To Do With It? would not be complete without mentioning the gift of receiving.

Many lovers, and loving people, and people who have loved many times, know nothing about receiving love from someone who loves them.

How easy it is for givers to give? They have given all their lives. However, when it comes to being able to receive, it is often a horse of a very different color. To givers, receiving feels vulnerable and unfamiliar. Receiving love requires losing control of the situation and giving up being in charge. It means sometimes, sitting back, *doing nothing* and saying "thank you".

Loving Is Knowing

How To Be

Treated Well

We mustn't rob our partners of the joy of giving. Letting someone give to you is a gift to them. Being treated well is a gracious state. Give love and receive love.

"One of the privileges I get in having a relationship with you is dreaming about ways to love you".

♥ ♥ ♥

EPILOGUE

The Long, Long Story... Continues

HE and SHE had grown in knowing each other. At first, she was the teacher and HE was the student. And, then, it switched. HE was the teacher. And SHE was the student. What SHE didn't know was that what HE had to teach her, was the gift of receiving. This meant that SHE had to learn to receive.

HE would often have to remind her, that HE was around and that SHE could ask him for assistance. SHE had to let him be a part of her life by letting him participate. SHE didn't have to do it "all" by herself anymore. And in fact, when she took over the show, SHE robbed him of the joy of giving.

So, SHE washed the lettuce and HE tore it apart. SHE went to the table and HE pulled out her chair. SHE said, "thank you". TOGETHER, THEY shared the meal.

And THEY shared life.

And THEY lived happily.

♥ ♥ ♥

AUTHOR'S POSTSCRIPT

As I sat at my computer typing out the last few pages, I paused a moment and picked up a pair of chinese medicine balls with my hand.

As I was practicing the technique of revolving the balls, first clockwise, then counter-clockwise, the challenge was to rotate them without letting them touch one another. If this feat is accomplished, music is made.

In my hand, I held the secret to relationships. If we can rotate around another without touching and then reverse the motion and still not intrude or bump into the other, we too, make music.

The music is not heard without the rotation of the two, independently, together. So too, with male and female. We are more when we are together, than when we are alone.